The Master's Blueprint

A Guide to Excelling As A Worshipful Master in Freemasonry

Michael Dawson

The Master's Blueprint

DEDICATION

To all the past, present, and future Worshipful Masters who have dedicated their time, energy, and passion to the noble work of leading their lodges, this book is dedicated to you.

We are grateful for your commitment to the principles of Freemasonry and for your tireless efforts in building stronger, more vibrant communities through your work in the lodge.

May this guide serve as a helpful resource and source of inspiration for all those who seek to follow in your footsteps and lead with wisdom, compassion, and integrity.

Thank you for your service and dedication to the craft.

TABLE OF CONTENTS

Understanding the Role of the Worshipful Master

The role of the Worshipful Master in a Masonic lodge is an important one. It is the highest position in the lodge and comes with significant responsibilities. In this chapter, we will explore the role of the Worshipful Master, including its historical context, the duties and responsibilities of the position, and the qualities that make for a successful leader.

Historical Context

The origins of the role of the Worshipful Master can be traced back to the medieval stonemasons' guilds. At that time, the Worshipful Master was the head of the guild and was responsible for overseeing the work of the other members, including apprentices and journeymen. As Freemasonry evolved, the role of the Worshipful Master also evolved, but its central purpose remained the same: to lead the lodge and ensure that it operates in accordance with Masonic principles and values.

Duties and Responsibilities

The duties and responsibilities of the Worshipful Master are numerous and varied. Some of the key responsibilities include:

1. Presiding over lodge meetings: The Worshipful Master is responsible for ensuring that lodge meetings are conducted in accordance with Masonic protocol and that all members have an opportunity to participate in the proceedings.

2. Setting the agenda: The Worshipful Master sets the agenda for each lodge meeting, ensuring that all necessary business is addressed and that any special events or guest speakers are scheduled.

3.   Appointing officers: The Worshipful Master appoints officers for the term and is responsible for ensuring that they understand their duties and responsibilities.

4.   Conducting degree work: The Worshipful Master is responsible for ensuring that all degree work is conducted in accordance with Masonic ritual and that candidates are properly prepared for initiation.

5.   Leading the lodge: The Worshipful Master is responsible for leading the lodge and ensuring that it operates in accordance with Masonic principles and values.

<u>Qualities of a Successful Worshipful Master</u>

To be a successful Worshipful Master, there are certain qualities that one should possess. These include:

1.   Strong leadership skills: The Worshipful Master should be a strong leader who can inspire and motivate others to achieve their best.

2.   Good communication skills: The Worshipful Master should be able to communicate effectively with lodge members, officers, and other stakeholders.

3.   In-depth knowledge of Masonic principles and values: The Worshipful Master should have a deep understanding of Masonic principles and values and be able to apply them in practice.

4.   Diplomacy and tact: The Worshipful Master should be diplomatic and tactful when dealing with sensitive or contentious issues.

5.   Commitment to the lodge: The Worshipful Master should be committed to the lodge and willing to put in the time and effort required to lead it effectively.

The role of the Worshipful Master is a crucial one in a Masonic lodge. The Worshipful Master is responsible for ensuring that the lodge operates in accordance with Masonic principles and values and for leading the lodge to achieve its goals. To be a successful Worshipful Master, one must possess strong leadership skills, good communication skills, in-depth knowledge of Masonic principles and values, diplomacy and tact, and a strong commitment to the lodge.

Preparing for Your Term: Planning and Goal-Setting

As a newly elected Worshipful Master, one of your first tasks is to begin preparing for your term. This includes setting goals and developing a plan to achieve them. In this chapter, we will explore the importance of planning and goal-setting, and provide practical tips and strategies for developing a successful plan for your term.

Why Planning and Goal-Setting Are Important

Effective planning and goal-setting are critical to the success of any organization, including a Masonic lodge. Without a clear plan and goals to work towards, it can be difficult to stay focused and motivated, and progress may be slow or nonexistent.

By taking the time to plan and set goals for your term, you can:

1.   Establish priorities: Setting goals helps you identify the most important priorities for your term and focus your efforts on achieving them.

2.   Stay organized: Planning your term allows you to stay organized and track your progress towards your goals.

3.   Measure success: Setting measurable goals allows you to track your progress and measure your success throughout your term.

4.   Create a sense of direction: Planning and goal-setting give you and your officers a sense of direction and purpose, helping you to work together towards a common goal.

<u>Developing a Plan</u>

To develop a successful plan for your term, there are several steps you should follow:

1.   Review the lodge's bylaws: Review the lodge's bylaws to ensure that you are familiar with the rules and regulations that govern the lodge and that you are fulfilling all of your obligations as Worshipful Master.

2.   Set priorities: Identify the most important priorities for your term, such as membership growth, fundraising, or community outreach.

3.   Set goals: Develop specific, measurable goals for each priority area. For example, if your priority is membership growth, you might set a goal to increase membership by 10% by the end of your term.

4.   Develop strategies: Develop strategies to achieve each goal, such as holding a membership drive, developing a social media campaign, or partnering with local organizations to increase visibility.

5.   Assign responsibilities: Assign responsibilities to officers and committee members, and ensure that everyone understands their roles and responsibilities.

6.   Develop a timeline: Develop a timeline for each goal, including key milestones and deadlines.

7.   Monitor progress: Regularly monitor progress towards your goals, and make adjustments as needed.

Tips and Strategies for Success

To ensure that your planning and goal-setting efforts are successful, here are some tips and strategies to keep in mind:

1. Involve others: Involve your officers and committee members in the planning process to ensure that everyone is invested in the goals and strategies.

2. Be realistic: Set goals that are challenging but achievable, and be realistic about the resources and time available to you.

3. Celebrate successes: Celebrate successes along the way, and use them as motivation to continue working towards your goals.

4. Be flexible: Be prepared to make adjustments to your plan as needed, based on feedback and changing circumstances.

Effective planning and goal-setting are essential to the success of any Masonic lodge. By taking the time to develop a clear plan and set goals for your term, you can establish priorities, stay organized, measure success, and create a sense of direction for your lodge. By following the steps outlined in this chapter and incorporating these tips and strategies, you can set your lodge on a path towards success and achieve your goals.

What are your goals for your term as master of your lodge?

What is your plan to attain your goals for your term as master of your lodge?

Building Strong Relationships within the Lodge

As the Worshipful Master of a Masonic lodge, one of your most important tasks is to build and maintain strong relationships with the members of your lodge. These relationships are the foundation of a successful and thriving lodge, and they are essential for creating a sense of community and unity among members. In this chapter, we will explore the importance of building strong relationships within the lodge and provide practical tips and strategies for doing so.

<u>Why Building Strong Relationships is Important</u>

Strong relationships are critical to the success of a Masonic lodge for several reasons:

1.   Unity: Building strong relationships among members creates a sense of unity within the lodge, which is essential for working together towards common goals and achieving success.

2.   Brotherhood: Masonry is founded on the principles of brotherhood, and building strong relationships among members helps to reinforce this important aspect of the craft.

3.   Support: Strong relationships within the lodge provide a sense of support and camaraderie among members, which can be especially important during difficult times.

4.   Retention: Members are more likely to stay active in the lodge if they feel a sense of connection and belonging, which is facilitated by strong relationships.

Tips and Strategies for Building Strong Relationships

Here are some practical tips and strategies for building strong relationships within the lodge:

1.   Communication: Communication is key to building strong relationships. Encourage open and honest communication among members, and make sure that everyone has an opportunity to share their thoughts and ideas.

2.   Social Events: Plan social events and activities outside of regular lodge meetings to give members an opportunity to connect on a personal level. This could include picnics, barbecues, game nights, or other activities that promote social interaction.

3.   Mentorship: Encourage mentorship programs within the lodge, where more experienced members can provide guidance and support to newer members. This helps to create a sense of connection and fosters a culture of learning and growth.

4.   Recognition: Recognize the contributions of individual members and the lodge as a whole. This could include awards or certificates of recognition, or simply acknowledging achievements and milestones during lodge meetings.

5.   Diversity and Inclusion: Ensure that all members feel included and valued within the lodge, regardless of their background or personal characteristics. Create a culture of diversity and inclusion that celebrates differences and encourages unity.

6.   Collaboration: Encourage collaboration among members and committees within the lodge. This helps to build relationships and creates a sense of shared ownership and investment in the success of the lodge.

Building strong relationships within the lodge is essential for creating a sense of unity, brotherhood, and support among members. By incorporating these tips and strategies into your leadership approach, you can foster a culture of communication, mentorship, recognition, diversity and inclusion, collaboration, and social connection. By doing so, you can create a thriving and successful lodge that is welcoming and inclusive for all members.

Navigating Masonic Etiquette and Protocol

As the Worshipful Master of a Masonic lodge, it is important to understand and follow the proper etiquette and protocol of Masonry. Masonic etiquette and protocol are based on centuries-old traditions and customs, and they help to maintain the integrity and dignity of the craft. In this chapter, we will explore the key aspects of Masonic etiquette and protocol, including dress code, behavior, and ceremonial procedures.

Dress Code

Proper attire is an essential part of Masonic etiquette. Masonic dress code varies depending on the type of event and the level of formality, but generally, the following guidelines apply:

1.   Lodge Meetings: Dress should be conservative and respectful. A dark suit or jacket and tie is appropriate for most meetings.

2.   Ceremonies: Formal dress is required for most ceremonies, including black tie or formal attire for installations and other major events.

3.   Degrees: For initiation and degree ceremonies, candidates should wear a plain white shirt and dark pants, with no jewelry or other adornments.

Behavior

Masonic etiquette also includes proper behavior during meetings and other events. Here are some key aspects of Masonic behavior:

1.   Respect: Members should show respect to the Worshipful Master, officers, and fellow members at all times.

2.   Punctuality: Members should arrive on time for meetings and events, and should not leave early without prior permission.

3.   Silence and Decorum: Members should maintain silence and decorum during meetings, ceremonies, and other events, and should not engage in distracting or disruptive behavior.

4.   Honesty: Members should be honest and truthful in their interactions with other members and in their duties within the lodge.

Ceremonial Procedures

Masonic ceremonies are steeped in tradition and follow a strict set of procedures and protocols. As the Worshipful Master, it is important to understand and follow these procedures to maintain the integrity and dignity of the craft. Here are some key aspects of ceremonial procedures:

1.   Order of Business: Lodge meetings should follow a set order of business, which typically includes opening and closing ceremonies, the reading of minutes, and the handling of lodge business.

2.   Ritual Work: Ritual work should be conducted according to the proper script and procedures, with proper attention given to pacing, tone, and delivery.

3.   Voting: Voting on lodge business should be conducted according to proper Masonic procedure, with members voting in accordance with their conscience and without fear or coercion.

4.   Ceremonial Attire: During degree ceremonies, candidates should wear the appropriate attire, and all officers should wear the appropriate regalia.

Masonic etiquette and protocol are essential aspects of the craft that help to maintain its integrity and dignity. As the Worshipful Master, it is important to understand and follow these customs and traditions, including proper dress code, behavior, and ceremonial procedures. By doing so, you can create a respectful and dignified atmosphere within your lodge, and help to maintain the traditions and customs of the craft for future generations.

Communicating Effectively as the Lodge Leader

As the Worshipful Master of a Masonic lodge, effective communication is an essential skill that will help you to lead your lodge successfully. Effective communication involves the ability to express your ideas, thoughts, and feelings clearly and to listen actively to others. In this chapter, we will explore the key aspects of effective communication and how to implement them within your lodge.

1. <u>Active Listening</u>

Active listening is a fundamental aspect of effective communication. It involves fully concentrating on what the other person is saying, understanding their message, and responding appropriately. As the Worshipful Master, you will be required to listen actively to the concerns and ideas of your lodge members, and respond with empathy and respect. Here are some tips for active listening:

Make eye contact with the speaker

Give your full attention to the speaker

Avoid interrupting the speaker

Clarify what the speaker is saying by summarizing their message

Respond with empathy and respect

2. <u>Clear and Concise Communication</u>

Clear and concise communication is essential to ensure that your lodge members understand your message. As the Worshipful Master, you will need to communicate clearly and concisely during lodge meetings and other events. Here are some tips for clear and concise communication:

Use simple language that is easy to understand

Avoid using jargon or technical terms that may confuse your audience

Use examples to illustrate your points

Speak at a moderate pace and volume

Encourage questions and feedback to ensure understanding

3. <u>Nonverbal Communication</u>

Nonverbal communication involves the use of body language, facial expressions, and gestures to convey your message. As the Worshipful Master, you will need to be aware of your nonverbal communication and how it may impact your audience. Here are some tips for effective nonverbal communication:

Maintain eye contact with your audience

Use appropriate facial expressions to convey your message

Use gestures to emphasize your message

Avoid fidgeting or other distracting behaviors

4. <u>Written Communication</u>

Written communication is another important aspect of effective communication. As the Worshipful Master, you may need to communicate with your lodge members through written messages such as newsletters, emails, and other correspondence. Here are some tips for effective written communication:

Use clear and concise language

Use appropriate formatting and structure

Address your audience appropriately

Provide clear and concise instructions

5. <u>Conflict Resolution</u>

Conflict resolution is an important aspect of effective communication. As the Worshipful Master, you may need to resolve conflicts between lodge members or between the lodge and other organizations. Here are some tips for effective conflict resolution:

Listen actively to both sides of the conflict

Identify the root cause of the conflict

Work with both parties to find a solution

Encourage compromise and collaboration

Effective communication is an essential skill for any successful Worshipful Master. By implementing these key aspects of effective communication, including active listening, clear and concise communication, nonverbal communication, written communication, and conflict resolution, you can create a respectful and productive atmosphere within your lodge, and help to ensure the success of your term as Worshipful Master.

Leading with Confidence and Authority

As the Worshipful Master of a Masonic lodge, you have been entrusted with the responsibility of leading your lodge towards its goals and objectives. This can be a daunting task, but it is essential that you lead with confidence and authority. In this chapter, we will explore the key aspects of leading with confidence and authority and how to implement them within your lodge.

1. <u>Knowledge and Expertise</u>

One of the most important ways to lead with confidence and authority is to have a strong foundation of knowledge and expertise. This means that you should have a deep understanding of the history, values, and traditions of the Masonic fraternity, as well as the roles and responsibilities of the Worshipful Master. It is also important to keep yourself up-to-date on the latest developments in Masonic practices and procedures. This will give you the confidence and authority to make informed decisions and to guide your lodge towards success.

2. <u>Clarity of Vision and Goals</u>

Another important aspect of leading with confidence and authority is having a clear vision and goals for your lodge. This involves identifying the strengths and weaknesses of your lodge and developing a plan to improve and enhance its performance. As the Worshipful Master, you should communicate your vision and goals clearly to your lodge members, and engage them in the process of achieving these objectives. This will help to create a shared sense of purpose and a sense of pride in the accomplishments of the lodge.

3.   Decisiveness and Assertiveness

Leadership requires decisiveness and assertiveness in making tough decisions and taking action when necessary. As the Worshipful Master, you will need to make decisions that may not always be popular or easy. It is important to approach these decisions with confidence and assertiveness, and to communicate your rationale clearly to your lodge members. This will help to build trust and respect among your members, and will demonstrate your ability to lead with confidence and authority.

4.   Confidence in Public Speaking

Public speaking is an essential skill for any successful leader. As the Worshipful Master, you will be required to speak in public at lodge meetings, special events, and other occasions. It is important to develop your public speaking skills to communicate your message clearly and effectively. This involves practicing your speeches, using appropriate body language, and engaging your audience with anecdotes and stories.

5.   Humility and Servant Leadership

Finally, it is important to remember that leading with confidence and authority does not mean being arrogant or dismissive of others. Humility and servant leadership are essential aspects of effective leadership. This involves being approachable and open to feedback from your lodge members, and working with them to achieve common goals. This will help to create a sense of community and shared purpose within your lodge, and will strengthen your authority as a leader.

Leading with confidence and authority requires a strong foundation of knowledge and expertise, a clear vision and goals, decisiveness and assertiveness, confidence in public speaking, and humility and servant leadership. By implementing these key aspects of leadership within your lodge, you can build trust and respect among your members, create a sense of shared purpose, and lead your lodge towards success.

Fostering a Culture of Inclusivity and Diversity

As the Worshipful Master of a Masonic lodge, it is important to foster a culture of inclusivity and diversity within your lodge. This means creating an environment where all members, regardless of their race, gender, religion, or background, feel welcome and valued. In this chapter, we will explore the key aspects of creating a culture of inclusivity and diversity, and how to implement them within your lodge.

1.   Understanding Inclusivity and Diversity

The first step in fostering a culture of inclusivity and diversity is to understand what these concepts mean. Inclusivity refers to creating an environment where everyone feels welcome and valued, regardless of their differences. Diversity refers to the differences among people, including their race, gender, religion, and background. By understanding these concepts, you can create a culture where everyone feels included and valued.

2.   Embracing Differences

Once you understand the importance of inclusivity and diversity, it is essential to embrace these differences. This means acknowledging and celebrating the unique contributions that each member brings to the lodge, and creating opportunities for them to share their experiences and perspectives. By embracing differences, you can create a culture where all members feel valued and appreciated.

3.   Educating Members

Education is an essential aspect of fostering a culture of inclusivity and diversity. This involves providing educational opportunities for members to learn about different cultures, religions, and backgrounds. It also means promoting open dialogue and discussion about sensitive topics related to diversity and inclusivity. By educating members, you can create a culture of respect and understanding.

4. Creating Inclusive Policies

Creating inclusive policies is another important aspect of fostering a culture of inclusivity and diversity. This includes policies that promote equality, fairness, and respect for all members. It also means creating policies that promote diversity and inclusion in all aspects of lodge activities, from membership to leadership positions. By creating inclusive policies, you can demonstrate your commitment to creating a culture where all members feel welcome and valued.

5. Leading by Example

Finally, it is important to lead by example when it comes to fostering a culture of inclusivity and diversity. This involves modeling inclusive behavior and language, and promoting diversity and inclusion in all aspects of lodge activities. It also means addressing any instances of discrimination or bias that may arise, and working to create a culture where all members feel respected and valued.

Fostering a culture of inclusivity and diversity is an essential aspect of being a successful and effective Worshipful Master. By understanding inclusivity and diversity, embracing differences, educating members, creating inclusive policies, and leading by example, you can create a culture where all members feel welcome and valued. This will not only strengthen your lodge, but also the Masonic fraternity as a whole, by promoting the values of equality, fairness, and respect for all.

Managing Finances and Fundraising for the Lodge

As a Worshipful Master, you are responsible for managing the finances of your lodge. This includes creating a budget, managing expenses, and fundraising to support lodge activities. In this chapter, we will explore the key aspects of managing finances and fundraising for the lodge, and how to implement them effectively.

1. <u>Creating a Budget</u>

The first step in managing lodge finances is to create a budget. A budget is a plan that outlines the expected income and expenses for the lodge. It helps to ensure that the lodge's financial resources are used effectively and efficiently. When creating a budget, it is important to consider all income sources, including membership dues, donations, and event proceeds. Expenses should be categorized, such as administrative costs, program expenses, and charitable donations. By creating a budget, you can ensure that the lodge's finances are well-managed.

2. <u>Managing Expenses</u>

Once you have created a budget, it is important to manage expenses effectively. This involves monitoring expenses regularly to ensure that they align with the budget. It also means prioritizing expenses and allocating funds appropriately. When managing expenses, it is important to keep accurate records of all transactions, including receipts, invoices, and bank statements. This helps to ensure that the lodge's finances are transparent and accountable.

3.   Fundraising

Fundraising is an essential aspect of managing lodge finances. Fundraising involves generating additional income for the lodge through events, donations, and sponsorships. When fundraising, it is important to be strategic and targeted. This means identifying potential donors and sponsors, creating compelling fundraising messages, and organizing events that align with the lodge's values and goals. It is also important to acknowledge and thank donors for their contributions. By effectively fundraising, you can support the lodge's activities and initiatives.

4.   Grant Writing

In addition to fundraising, grant writing is another way to secure financial resources for the lodge. Grant writing involves researching and identifying grant opportunities, preparing grant applications, and submitting them to potential grantors. Grant writing requires strong writing skills, attention to detail, and knowledge of the grant process. By securing grants, the lodge can fund specific programs and initiatives, and support the local community.

5.   Financial Accountability

Finally, financial accountability is an essential aspect of managing lodge finances. This means being transparent and accountable in all financial transactions. It also means creating financial reports that are accurate, timely, and informative. When presenting financial reports, it is important to provide context and explain any discrepancies or significant changes. By maintaining financial accountability, you can demonstrate the lodge's commitment to responsible financial management.

Managing finances and fundraising are essential aspects of being a successful and effective Worshipful Master. By creating a budget, managing expenses, fundraising, writing grants, and maintaining financial accountability, you can ensure that the lodge's financial resources are well-managed and support the lodge's activities and initiatives. Effective financial management also promotes transparency, accountability, and trust among members and the community. By implementing these key strategies, you can ensure that the lodge's financial resources are used effectively and efficiently.

Conducting Effective Lodge Meetings

One of the most important responsibilities of a Worshipful Master is to conduct effective lodge meetings. Lodge meetings provide an opportunity for members to come together, discuss lodge business, and make important decisions. In this chapter, we will explore the key aspects of conducting effective lodge meetings, and how to implement them effectively.

1.   <u>Setting the Agenda</u>

The first step in conducting effective lodge meetings is to set the agenda. The agenda should be prepared in advance and distributed to all members. The agenda should include items such as opening and closing ceremonies, reports from officers and committees, old and new business, and any special presentations or events. The agenda should be structured in a way that allows for timely and effective discussion and decision-making.

2.   <u>Conducting the Meeting</u>

Once the agenda is set, it is important to conduct the meeting in a structured and organized manner. This involves following parliamentary procedure, which is a set of rules for conducting meetings effectively. Parliamentary procedure ensures that meetings are conducted fairly and efficiently, and that all members have an opportunity to participate. The Worshipful Master should be familiar with parliamentary procedure and be able to guide the meeting effectively.

3.   <u>Facilitating Discussion</u>

During the meeting, it is important to facilitate discussion effectively. This involves encouraging participation from all members, managing time effectively, and ensuring that discussion stays on topic. The Worshipful Master should also be able to manage conflict effectively and ensure that all members are respectful and courteous to one another.

4. <u>Making Decisions</u>

At the end of the meeting, it is important to make decisions effectively. This involves ensuring that all members have a chance to express their opinions and vote on decisions. The Worshipful Master should ensure that decisions are made democratically and that all members are informed of the outcome.

5. <u>Following Up</u>

Finally, it is important to follow up after the meeting. This involves ensuring that all decisions are implemented effectively, and that any action items are assigned and completed. The Worshipful Master should also ensure that minutes of the meeting are taken and distributed to all members in a timely manner.

Conducting effective lodge meetings is an essential aspect of being a successful and effective Worshipful Master. By setting the agenda, conducting the meeting in a structured and organized manner, facilitating discussion effectively, making decisions democratically, and following up, you can ensure that lodge meetings are productive, efficient, and respectful. Effective lodge meetings also promote transparency, accountability, and trust among members and the community. By implementing these key strategies, you can ensure that the lodge's activities and initiatives are well-supported and successful.

Organizing and Planning Lodge Events

One of the primary ways in which lodges engage with their communities and members is through the organization of events. Whether it be charity fundraisers, community service projects, or social events, effective event planning is crucial for the success of the lodge. In this chapter, we will explore the key aspects of organizing and planning lodge events, and how to implement them effectively.

1.   Establishing Goals and Objectives

The first step in organizing and planning lodge events is to establish clear goals and objectives. These goals should be aligned with the lodge's overall mission and vision. For example, if the lodge's mission is to serve the community, an event goal might be to raise funds for a local charity. By establishing clear goals and objectives, the planning process can be focused, and resources can be allocated effectively.

2.   Developing a Planning Committee

Once the goals and objectives have been established, it is important to develop a planning committee. The committee should include members with diverse skill sets and should be led by a member who is responsible for overseeing the planning process. The planning committee should be responsible for establishing the event budget, developing event timelines, and coordinating with vendors and other stakeholders.

3.   Budgeting and Fundraising

Event planning often requires significant financial resources. Therefore, it is important to establish a budget and fundraising plan early in the planning process. The planning committee should develop a comprehensive budget that includes all anticipated expenses, such as venue rental fees, catering costs, and marketing expenses. The committee should also explore fundraising opportunities, such as sponsorships and ticket sales, to offset these costs.

4.   Selecting a Venue

The selection of a venue is a crucial aspect of event planning. The venue should be chosen based on the event's objectives, the size of the event, and the location. The planning committee should consider factors such as accessibility, parking, and the availability of amenities such as audiovisual equipment and catering services. The venue should also be chosen in accordance with the event's budget.

5.   Marketing and Promotion

Effective marketing and promotion are essential for the success of any event. The planning committee should develop a comprehensive marketing plan that includes social media, email marketing, and traditional advertising channels. The plan should also include a timeline for when each marketing activity will be executed. The goal is to generate excitement and interest in the event, and to attract as many attendees as possible.

6.   Day-Of Coordination

On the day of the event, it is important to have a dedicated team of volunteers who are responsible for event coordination. These volunteers should be assigned specific roles, such as registration, hospitality, and logistics. The planning committee should also establish a communication plan to ensure that everyone is on the same page and that any issues can be addressed quickly.

Organizing and planning lodge events requires a comprehensive approach that encompasses budgeting, fundraising, venue selection, marketing, and day-of coordination. By establishing clear goals and objectives, developing a planning committee, budgeting and fundraising effectively, selecting a suitable venue, marketing and promoting the event, and coordinating effectively on the day of the event, you can ensure that your lodge's events are well-organized and successful. Effective event planning also provides an opportunity to engage with the community, build relationships with members, and promote the lodge's values and mission. By implementing these key strategies, you can ensure that your lodge's events are impactful and meaningful.

What lodge events do you have planned for your year?

Embracing Technology and Innovation in Freemasonry

Freemasonry is an ancient organization that has a rich history of tradition and ritual. However, as the world becomes increasingly digital and interconnected, it is crucial for lodges to embrace technology and innovation to remain relevant and engage with younger generations. In this chapter, we will explore the benefits of embracing technology and innovation in Freemasonry, as well as some of the challenges and considerations.

1.   <u>Benefits of Embracing Technology and Innovation</u>

There are several benefits to embracing technology and innovation in Freemasonry. Firstly, technology can help lodges to streamline administrative tasks such as membership management, event planning, and financial reporting. This allows for more efficient use of time and resources, and frees up members to focus on more meaningful activities such as ritual work and community engagement.

Secondly, technology can also help lodges to engage with younger generations who are more digitally-savvy and expect a certain level of technological integration in their organizations. By embracing technology, lodges can reach out to younger members and provide them with a platform to connect with other members, learn about Masonic history and tradition, and participate in lodge activities.

Finally, technology can also help lodges to promote Masonic values and mission to a wider audience. Through social media, websites, and other digital channels, lodges can share their message with the community and engage with potential new members.

2.   Challenges and Considerations

Despite the benefits of technology and innovation, there are also some challenges and considerations that lodges should be aware of. One of the main challenges is the potential for technology to detract from the traditional values and practices of Freemasonry. As such, it is important to find a balance between embracing technology and maintaining the core values of the organization.

Another consideration is the potential for technology to widen the gap between generations within the lodge. Older members who are less comfortable with technology may feel left behind, while younger members may feel frustrated with outdated systems and processes. Therefore, it is important to ensure that technology is implemented in a way that is accessible and user-friendly for all members.

3.   Ways to Embrace Technology and Innovation

There are several ways in which lodges can embrace technology and innovation. Firstly, lodges can invest in software and platforms that can help to streamline administrative tasks such as membership management and event planning. This frees up time and resources for more meaningful activities such as community engagement and ritual work.

Secondly, lodges can create a website and social media presence to promote Masonic values and engage with potential new members. This provides an opportunity to share information about the lodge's history, values, and activities, and to connect with a wider audience.

Finally, lodges can also explore innovative approaches to ritual work and community engagement. For example, virtual ceremonies and events can provide a way to connect with members who are unable to attend in-person, while new community engagement initiatives can help to promote Masonic values and build relationships with the community.

Embracing technology and innovation in Freemasonry can bring many benefits, including increased efficiency, engagement with younger generations, and wider promotion of Masonic values and mission. However, it is important to find a balance between embracing technology and maintaining the core values and traditions of the organization. By investing in software and platforms to streamline administrative tasks, creating a digital presence to engage with the wider community, and exploring innovative approaches to ritual work and community engagement, lodges can embrace technology and innovation in a way that is respectful of the organization's history and values while remaining relevant and engaging with younger generations.

Managing Conflict and Resolving Disputes within the Lodge

Conflict and disputes can arise in any organization, including within a Masonic lodge. It is important for lodge leaders to have a plan in place to manage conflict and resolve disputes in a way that is respectful, fair, and in line with Masonic values. In this chapter, we will explore strategies for managing conflict and resolving disputes within the lodge.

1.   Understanding the Causes of Conflict

Before we can effectively manage conflict and resolve disputes, it is important to understand the causes of conflict within the lodge. Some common causes of conflict include differences in opinion or values, misunderstandings, power struggles, and personal issues. It is important for lodge leaders to be aware of these potential causes of conflict and to take steps to address them when they arise.

2.   Developing Conflict Management Strategies

One effective way to manage conflict within the lodge is to develop a conflict management strategy. This strategy should outline the steps that will be taken when conflict arises, including who will be involved in the process and how disputes will be resolved. Lodge leaders should also consider establishing a code of conduct or behavioral standards for members, which can help to prevent conflicts before they occur.

3.   Encouraging Open Communication

Effective communication is essential for managing conflict within the lodge. Lodge leaders should encourage open and honest communication among members, and provide opportunities for members to share their thoughts and concerns.

This can be done through regular lodge meetings, one-on-one conversations, and group discussions.

4.   <u>Seeking Mediation and Arbitration</u>

In some cases, disputes may require outside mediation or arbitration to be resolved. Lodge leaders should have a plan in place for seeking mediation or arbitration when needed, and should work with a qualified mediator or arbitrator to ensure that disputes are resolved in a fair and impartial manner.

5.   <u>Resolving Disputes through Masonic Principles</u>

Masonic principles provide a framework for resolving disputes within the lodge. These principles include the importance of harmony, justice, and brotherly love. Lodge leaders should encourage members to approach conflicts with these principles in mind, and work to resolve disputes in a way that is respectful and fair to all parties involved.

6.   <u>Encouraging Forgiveness and Reconciliation</u>

Finally, it is important for lodge leaders to encourage forgiveness and reconciliation when conflicts are resolved. Lodge members should be encouraged to forgive one another and to work towards rebuilding trust and repairing damaged relationships. This can be done through group discussions, personal conversations, and other forms of communication.

Conflict and disputes can be challenging to manage within any organization, including a Masonic lodge. However, by understanding the causes of conflict, developing a conflict management strategy, encouraging open communication, seeking mediation and arbitration when necessary, resolving disputes through Masonic principles, and encouraging for-giveness and reconciliation, lodge leaders can effectively manage conflict and resolve disputes in a way that is respect-ful, fair, and in line with Masonic values.

Mentoring and Developing Future Lodge Leaders

One of the most important responsibilities of a Worshipful Master in Freemasonry is to mentor and develop future lodge leaders. The success and continuity of the lodge depend on the quality and commitment of its leaders, and it is the role of the Worshipful Master to ensure that these leaders are identified, trained, and supported. In this chapter, we will explore strategies for mentoring and developing future lodge leaders.

1.   <u>Identifying Potential Leaders</u>

The first step in mentoring and developing future lodge leaders is to identify those members who have the potential to become effective leaders. This can be done through observation, conversations, and other forms of communication. Lodge leaders should look for members who are committed to the values of Freemasonry, demonstrate leadership potential, and have a strong desire to serve the lodge and its members.

2.   <u>Providing Leadership Opportunities</u>

Once potential leaders have been identified, it is important to provide them with opportunities to develop their leadership skills. This can be done by assigning them to leadership roles within the lodge, such as committee chairs, officers, or mentors to newer members. These leadership opportunities should be tailored to the individual's strengths and areas for growth, and should provide them with opportunities to learn and practice leadership skills in a supportive environment.

3.   <u>Offering Training and Development Programs</u>

Lodge leaders should also offer training and development programs to help future leaders develop their skills and knowledge. These programs can include workshops, seminars, or online courses, and should cover topics such as leadership, communication, conflict resolution, and Masonic history and philosophy. Providing ongoing education and training opportunities will help future leaders to grow and develop, and ensure that they have the skills and knowledge necessary to lead the lodge effectively.

4.   <u>Providing Feedback and Support</u>

As future leaders develop their skills and knowledge, it is important for current leaders to provide them with feedback and support. This can include regular check-ins, feedback on their performance, and guidance on how to improve their leadership skills. Lodge leaders should also be available to provide support and advice when future leaders encounter challenges or difficulties in their roles.

5.   <u>Encouraging Mentorship and Collaboration</u>

Another important aspect of mentoring and developing future leaders is to encourage mentorship and collaboration among lodge members. Future leaders can benefit greatly from working with experienced leaders, and current leaders can benefit from the fresh ideas and perspectives of future leaders. Lodge leaders should encourage mentorship and collaboration through formal and informal programs, such as mentor-mentee pairings, leadership retreats, and team-building activities.

Mentoring and developing future lodge leaders is essential for the long-term success and continuity of the lodge. By identifying potential leaders, providing leadership opportunities, offering training and development programs, providing feedback and support, and encouraging mentorship and collaboration, lodge leaders can help to ensure that future leaders are well-prepared to lead the lodge effectively. With a strong and committed group of future leaders, the lodge can continue to thrive and serve its members and community for years to come.

Navigating the Relationship between the Lodge and the Grand Lodge

As a Worshipful Master in Freemasonry, it is important to understand the relationship between your lodge and the Grand Lodge. The Grand Lodge is the governing body for Freemasonry within a particular jurisdiction, and provides guidance, support, and oversight for local lodges. In this chapter, we will explore strategies for navigating the relationship between the lodge and the Grand Lodge.

1. <u>Understanding the Role of the Grand Lodge</u>

The first step in navigating the relationship between the lodge and the Grand Lodge is to understand the role of the Grand Lodge. The Grand Lodge is responsible for setting and enforcing the rules and regulations that govern Freemasonry within a particular jurisdiction. The Grand Lodge also provides support and guidance to local lodges, and oversees the administration of Masonic degrees and rituals.

2. Building a Strong Relationship with the Grand Lodge

To navigate the relationship between the lodge and the Grand Lodge effectively, it is important to build a strong and positive relationship with the Grand Lodge. This can be done by attending Grand Lodge meetings and events, participating in Grand Lodge committees and programs, and communicating regularly with Grand Lodge officials. Building a strong relationship with the Grand Lodge will help to ensure that the lodge is well-informed about Grand Lodge policies and procedures, and that the Grand Lodge is aware of the needs and concerns of the local lodge.

3.   Following Grand Lodge Policies and Procedures

Another important aspect of navigating the relationship between the lodge and the Grand Lodge is to follow Grand Lodge policies and procedures. The Grand Lodge sets the rules and regulations that govern Freemasonry within a particular jurisdiction, and it is important for local lodges to abide by these rules. This can include policies related to membership, ritual, and financial management. By following Grand Lodge policies and procedures, the lodge can ensure that it is in compliance with Grand Lodge regulations, and that it is fulfilling its obligations to the broader Masonic community.

4.   Communicating with the Grand Lodge

Effective communication is essential for navigating the relationship between the lodge and the Grand Lodge. Lodge leaders should communicate regularly with Grand Lodge officials to ensure that they are well-informed about Grand Lodge policies and procedures, and to address any concerns or issues that may arise. Communication can take many forms, including phone calls, emails, and in-person meetings. Lodge leaders should also ensure that they are communicating effectively with their own lodge members about Grand Lodge policies and procedures, to ensure that everyone is on the same page.

5.   Participating in Grand Lodge Programs and Initiatives

Participating in Grand Lodge programs and initiatives can be an effective way to strengthen the relationship between the lodge and the Grand Lodge. The Grand Lodge often sponsors educational programs, leadership development initiatives, and community service projects, and local lodges can benefit greatly from participating in these programs. By participating in Grand Lodge programs and initiatives, the lodge can demonstrate its commitment to the broader Masonic community, and can benefit from the resources and support provided by the Grand Lodge.

Navigating the relationship between the lodge and the Grand Lodge is an essential part of being a successful Worshipful Master in Freemasonry. By understanding the role of the Grand Lodge, building a strong relationship with the Grand Lodge, following Grand Lodge policies and procedures, communicating effectively with the Grand Lodge, and participating in Grand Lodge programs and initiatives, lodge leaders can ensure that their lodge is well-supported and well-positioned to serve its members and community. With a positive and productive relationship with the Grand Lodge, the lodge can continue to thrive and uphold the values of Freemasonry for generations to come.

Reflecting on Your Term and Leaving a Lasting Legacy

As your term as Worshipful Master draws to a close, it is important to take some time to reflect on your accomplishments and the legacy you want to leave behind. Your leadership during your term has undoubtedly made a significant impact on the lodge and its members, and it is important to acknowledge and celebrate these achievements.

Reflecting on Your Accomplishments

One of the first steps in reflecting on your term is to take stock of what you have accomplished. This can be done by reviewing the goals you set at the beginning of your term and assessing how successful you were in achieving them. You should also consider any unexpected challenges that arose during your term and how you overcame them.

It can be helpful to gather feedback from lodge members on their perception of your leadership and the impact it had on the lodge. This can be done through surveys or informal discussions, and can provide valuable insights into the areas where you excelled and areas where there may be room for improvement.

Leaving a Lasting Legacy

As you reflect on your term, you should also consider the legacy you want to leave behind. What do you want the lodge to remember about your leadership and the impact you had? This may involve identifying areas where you made significant improvements and establishing systems or programs that will continue to benefit the lodge in the future.

One effective way to leave a lasting legacy is to establish a succession plan for future lodge leaders. This can involve identifying potential candidates for leadership positions and providing them with the support and guidance they need to succeed. Mentoring future leaders and providing them with opportunities to learn and grow can ensure that the lodge continues to thrive in the years to come.

Another way to leave a lasting legacy is to establish a charitable or community program that the lodge can support. This can involve identifying a cause or organization that aligns with the values of the lodge and providing ongoing support through fundraising, volunteering, or other means.

Finally, it is important to ensure that your term ends on a positive note. This can involve planning a special event or ceremony to celebrate the achievements of the lodge during your term and to recognize the contributions of lodge members. It can also involve ensuring a smooth transition for the incoming Worshipful Master, including providing them with all the necessary information and resources they need to succeed.

Reflecting on your term as Worshipful Master and leaving a lasting legacy can be a meaningful and rewarding experience. By taking the time to assess your accomplishments and plan for the future, you can ensure that your leadership has a lasting impact on the lodge and its members. Remember that your term is just one chapter in the long and rich history of the lodge, and that the work you do today will help to shape the future of the organization for generations to come.

This book is property of:

____

Member of Lodge:

____

Entered Apprentice Degree:

____

Fellowcraft Degree:

____

Master Mason Degree:

____

Installed as Master:

____